ON THE JOURNEY

ON THE JOURNEY
Poems of Betrayal and Hope

Elaine VandeReis

Gentle Path Press
P.O. Box 3172
Carefree, Arizona 85377
www.gentlepath.com
Copyright © 2018 by Gentle Path Press

First edition: 2018

For more information regarding our publications,
contact Gentle Path Press at
1-800-708-1796 (toll-free U.S. only)

ISBN: 978-1-7320673-0-1

Contents

Original Preface, April 2005.

Dear Friend,

I made this book for you.

The poetry within reflects my thoughts and feelings during the first year of my journey. The poems range from the utmost depths of rage and despair to the attainment of compassion and the decision to love, despite the risk. I hope that in them you will find some validation of feelings and experiences you have had, and that they will give voice to things that may have seemed too painful for words to express.

You will see that, while the poems vary in their hopefulness, there is some progression toward a more peaceful state of mind. The final poems are not an endpoint, however, but a way station. My journey is not over. Like you, I am still traveling, and I do not know where the path leads me.

You will also see that some poems reflect my struggle to hear the guidance of my Higher Power. My faith has been a very important factor in my recovery so far. I could not write about this journey without expressing my awareness of, and gratitude for His work in my life. Not everything I have said in these poems will apply to you, since each person's journey is unique. I ask that you bear with me, and take only what you wish to, from this book.

I am grateful to my friends from Saturday morning COSA who encouraged me to make this work available to others. Their kind words of support and validation mean more to me than I can say. I also thank my husband, for whom most of these were written and who was my original intended audience for all of them. His openness to hearing these often painful words and the devastating emotions they depict has deepened my appreciation for him.

EV

Preface, August 2017.

Dear Reader,

The original version of this book was shared bit by bit with COSA friends who expressed an interest. When I later shared this work with Dr. Barbara Levinson, she urged me to publish it, and kindly put me in touch with Dr. Stefanie Carnes and Gentle Path Press. I am very grateful for their encouragement and help in bringing this work to a wider audience.

The current version is divided into four sections, corresponding to different aspects and stages of my recovery journey. It contains new material, both in the form of new poetry, brief commentary, and introductions to the sections.

A great deal has happened since the first months of my journey, when much of this book was written. My perspective has changed over time as my recovery and my healing have gradually been realized. A group of additional poems were written over several years that reflect these changes, as I began to focus less on myself and my pain, and more on recovery and compassion. Many of these may be found in the final section, titled Downstream.

I hope these words will speak to your heart.

EV

I.

Discovery

In 2004, my world changed forever. I had been married for 25 years to my high school sweetheart. We had one child, then in her teens. We both worked, and we had a comfortable life. In June that year we celebrated our 25th anniversary with a vow renewal and a festive party for family and friends, followed by a "honeymoon" trip. My husband still traveled too much for work, but overall, things seemed to be going well.

In late September of that year I woke one morning in severe pain. I ended up in the Emergency Department of a hospital, driven there by my daughter who had gotten her driver's license only the day before. After many tests and much confusion, I was diagnosed with Pelvic Inflammatory Disease, secondary to a sexually transmitted infection. My husband came home from his trip early, after being convinced over the phone by our daughter that he really *must*, as mom was in the hospital. In the hospital room, he and I talked alone. I was sedated for the pain, and stunned by what I had been told. He confessed the general outlines of his sex addiction, which had been going on since before we even met. He expressed remorse and seemed genuinely horrified that his actions had placed me in this situation. At that time I couldn't even feel. The searing emotional pain would start later, once I was home again.

I began writing almost instinctively. I had to do something with the overwhelming pain and confusion I was feeling. Someone I had loved and trusted for decades had turned out to be someone else entirely! A person I had not only loved, but admired and deeply trusted, had betrayed me in what seemed the worst way possible. It felt as though all my assumptions about the world had been shattered. I no longer knew what was true, and what was false. What about all those years when we enjoyed life together? Was that all an illusion? What else in my world wasn't real? All my good memories of us were now poisoned. My history had vanished and I was in free fall.

One of the most disconcerting parts of this situation was that my husband shut down emotionally. From my perspective, if you had done something this immensely wrong to someone you were close to, wouldn't you be on your knees begging forgiveness? Wouldn't you be showing your remorse through your words and emotions? Instead he stolidly listened to my pain – doubtless very hard to do, at the time – saying very little and showing little emotion. I couldn't understand this. My apparent inability to reach him was another reason I began writing the poetry in this book. It was my way of trying to capture my experience in a way he could read and consider. Maybe, I thought, he can begin to understand the impact of what he's done.

What I know now but didn't know then, was that his shutting down did not mean he didn't realize the impact. It was as though his emotional system was an electrical circuit that had experienced a power surge in a thunderstorm: the circuit breaker flipped, the power went off and he shut down. I later learned that addicts are generally poor at handling strong emotions; after all, addictions serve to keep them from having to do so. Nevertheless, he did read all of the poems I wrote. He didn't always react, but he kept them in his drawer, and I later learned he read them over.

The first section of poems were written in the turbulence following discovery. They reflect the confusion, pain and trauma of that time. You will see metaphors reflecting my sense of physical violation at being made sick. You will see the swings of mood that characterize that time, from a desire to lash out in rage, to crushing sorrow, to a persistent love for my partner of many years. You will see the unwanted imagery and traumatic memories that haunted me, and my sense of alienation from my husband. You will also see my struggle with rage and disgust toward his acting out and his acting out partners. The poems also represent the sense that there is a struggle between darkness and light going on in this personal battle.

Hard to Swallow

First came the draught of sickness: It grew in my belly, an alien burden,
Till at last I bore it like a demon child.

Then came the dagger of revelation: swallowed whole, point first,
        its way eased by other pain.
I still bleed where it cut a path.

Then comprehension: A vast, cold lump
That burned my vitals as I forced it down my throat.

Sorrow came next: A burrowing worm.
Finding my heart congenial, it took up residence.
Now it seems there was no time when it was not there.

At last despair: A black, choking bile
That goes down like acid and comes back up as hate.
Its substance is darkness; its measure is death.

But of all the poisons that I took,
This was the worst:
That what I thought was sacred was profaned.

This was what it felt like to go through discovery. Illness, unwelcome knowledge and emotions, and the understanding that what I thought to be real was not.

Filleted

First, with the news: my guts kicked out.
Lying in bloody spirals on the floor, going the surgeons one better.
The blood will be cleaned up later;
The rest of me blends well with the white hospital walls.
Now the boning knife descends
   to take what remains of my spine.
It seems I won't be needing it now.
My female organs gone, taken with the rest,
Gone to offal in steaming piles.
No more need for procreation, then;
All of it can be disposed of.
The heart, too?
It beats on, pumping to nowhere.
Bereft of its accustomed role it slows, atrophies,
Then nothing more.

The loss of physical integrity, the violation of my body, left me feeling irretrievably damaged. I didn't know whether I would recover physically, at this point, or what other consequences there might be from my husband's acting out. I was angry, but also close to despair.

My Left Arm

Who would have guessed it?
Puncture wounds: numerous and bloody,
Surrounded by bruises purpling just under the skin.
Veins sunken, but visible as roadways against the whiteness.
Needles strapped down by tape,
Leading to tubes that draw life in and draw it out again.

This is the icon that draws you toward the light;
This is the very instrument of God.

Despite how it seemed to me at first, my husband was actually deeply affected by seeing me in the hospital, hooked up to multiple IVs. I had so many that they began putting IVs in odd places just to get a good vein. Consequently I was covered with bruises. The effect on him was to motivate him to begin recovery. As I would see however, it was not to be a straight road.

Questions

What is it you really wanted?
A collection of assorted body parts, pleasingly arranged;
Bags of saline propped up and protruding;
Empty spaces waiting to be filled,
      wide open for business.
Nothing, by the handful.

Partners are often baffled by the behavior of addicts. I certainly was. I couldn't understand why my husband would choose to act out as he did, with people for whom he manifestly cared nothing. This mentality, although I now understand it intellectually, has never made sense to me emotionally.

A View from the Moral High Ground

It's cold up here, and empty, too.
Someone stole my shelter,
     and now my light's gone out in this fierce, cold wind.
I can see for miles, but all I see is wasteland.
I thought you were with me,
     but I see that only my own tracks lead up here.
It is so tempting to go down where you must be.
Surely the wind does not blow so hard down there?
I stay, because this way only one of us is lost.
Maybe if I stay, in time you will find me,
     even in this night,
Where the only light there is comes from above.

Early in the journey it is easy to see oneself as the "good one", the person who didn't do the Bad Thing. It may well be true that the partner didn't do what the addict did, nevertheless it gets lonely up there on the moral high ground, and staying up there makes it awfully hard to connect.

Visions

You didn't think I'd see you, but I do.
I see you every day now;
Your hands grasping, fondling;
Your mouth greedily exploring;
Limbs entangled;
The hard, pumping wetness of your lust,
    conceived in fever, spent in darkness.
I see your face: slack, empty, thoughtless.
You don't see me; perhaps you never did.
I slip around corners now, shadowy, fading:
    invisible, even to myself.

Intrusive images are a frequent problem for partners. Even for those who didn't personally see anything happen, mental images can be a major source of pain. I am glad that I did not ask for too many specific details; it would only have made this worse.

Hidden

What did I see in you?
I am beginning to forget.
Each day your face is more and more obscured
        by the grimy overlay of fingerprints that cover your body.
Their stain does not wash off.
Soon your features will be blurred beyond recognition.
Then whom will I love?
I no longer know.

After discovery, the partner's changed view of the addict can lead to estrangement and emotional alienation. It is hard to go on hurting that much. Sometimes it feels easier to wall oneself off instead. In my case, the intrusive images covered up my former mental image of my husband. They literally obscured him from my view.

On Pain

Allow me to explain:
Pain is the direct result of things that harm us.
Suffering is our response to it.

When we experience pain,
God in His mercy can relieve our suffering, if we let Him.

I am not there yet, for my pain is too fresh, the wounds too deep.
Each day they are slashed open anew.

Now I know that Hell is not a place.
We all carry Hell within us, waiting to be realized.
This one is mine.

Early months after discovery are hell. There are no other words for it. I did a lot of praying during that time, but I couldn't let the peace in. I was in my own personal hell, and it seemed there was no escape.

The Depths

Your well's run dry.
Or maybe it was never very deep.
Shallow wells dry up when the seasons change,
      and they run to mud.

Mine goes down, deep below,
      where you have never been.
The waters there are cold and clear.

I think you never had the heart to plumb those depths.

Partners can be surprised and appalled by the apparent shallowness of the addict's attachment to them. How can it be, we ask ourselves, that I loved this person so much, and he cared for me so little? At this point in my journey I did not yet understand that when my husband acted out, he was in a kind of altered mental state in which he compartmentalized what he was doing, keeping it artificially separated from the rest of his life.

Legion

Too many to count, their numbers faze me.
Swarming like insects,
        they pass through in darkness.
They belong outside, but you let them in.
            Now I am reduced to living here with them.
            I open my lamp and watch them scuttle back to night;
I crush a few like roaches under my heel.

They are too many!
        And my light shines but dimly in the dark.

If as in my case your addict partner has acted out with many partners out-side the relationship, the concept of numbers can be overwhelming. For me, they were unwelcome intruders. The image of cockroaches also captures my sense of disgust.

Your face without my loving gaze grows indistinct.
I see you retreating from me,
Drawn by a hidden string that
  pulls you away into the far distance.
You grow smaller on my horizon,
  where once you stood a giant in my thoughts.
Now only your shadow looms large.
It shades my heart, and leaves me here to wonder
  where the light has gone.

I began withdrawing from my husband emotionally after a while. Life went on in some ways but my new image of him was so unacceptable that I couldn't feel close to him. At this point, I was not sure whether things would ever get better.

Freedom

If I were free
I would no longer have to worry about where you are
     and what you're doing.
If I were free
I would not have to hear the lie behind your words,
     every time you say you love me.
If I were free
I could find myself a good man,
     one whose hands are clean
And whose heart is not fouled with deception.

A number of COSA sisters have told me they felt exactly like this at some point. What if I try on the idea of being free? What if I no longer cared? What would it be like to start over?

Romantic Notions of the Day

Shall I compare thee to the bathroom floor?

**   **   **   **   **   **

How have you hurt me? Let me count the ways.

**   **   **   **   **   **

My love is like a red, red, sore.

**   **   **   **   **   **

Black, black, black is the color of my true love's heart.

**   **   **   **   **   **

Sometimes my prince will come, but not with me.

When sex addiction comes in the door, any romance goes out the window. This was my way of saying that any romantic illusions I might once have had were thoroughly destroyed.

Last Wishes

Before I die, just once, at least:
A night without sleepless agony;
Wakening without the sudden blow of deepest pain;
Rest without the contemplation of utter evil that brings
      constriction to my heart;
A day without the flashing trauma of unwelcome images;
A parting without the terrible burden of suspicion and distrust;
Thoughts that do not inevitably lead to the racing heart of fear;
Love, without the poisonous admixture of grief and loss;
Self-regard that does not end in loathing and despair;
Memories that are not tainted and defiled;
A future that leads from emptiness to light.

Months of intrusive images, flashbacks, triggers, along with a constant burden of grief and fear, had worn me down. I couldn't sleep well. I walked through my days like a robot. This was my prayer for some relief.

The stronger I get,
The weaker you look to me.
The less I worry about losing you,
The more I worry about losing me.

At a certain point I began to notice that focusing on my husband, the addict, made me feel worse, while focusing on myself and my recovery, made me feel better. For those of you long in recovery this will not come as a surprise, since this is exactly what 12-step teaches you. It just took me a while to really understand what it meant.

I know every line of your face.
I see your smile,
The small expressions that you make when you speak,
The tiredness in your face that I know from long acquaintance.

Every bit of you is dear to me; I cannot help but love you,
        no matter how much it hurts to do so.

My journey was complicated by the fact that I genuinely loved my husband, and he me. Neither of us wanted the relationship to end. It's just that loving him was so painful...

Serial Killer

Each time is different, and the same.
He finds her, someplace where he shouldn't be.

Getting ready to perform his act he lays out his instruments.
Do they glitter?
Not so much as he thinks.

The knife rises and falls: The cut is all his,
The bleeding is all mine.

I was still trying to comprehend how someone I had thought was good, could be involved in such evil. The metaphor of the serial killer brings to mind the effect of his actions on me.

Sleep soundly,
Like the innocent or the dead.
Which are you?

Watching my husband sleep, I could not help but wonder how he could sleep at all, with the burden of shame and guilt he must have. At the time, I assumed he must not really feel bad about it. Now I realize that his ability to compartmentalize was what allowed him to survive.

Circle

I hate you, and I hope you die.

No, no, maybe I hope you live,
        so you can suffer, just like I do.

No, wait.
Now that I see your face in front of me,
I remember how I've loved you, and I feel pity for you.
I want you to get well.
It breaks my heart to see you.

Then I recall how much it cost Him to die for us.
I remember how His forgiveness covers all our transgressions;
Yes, even yours.
Even yours.

Yours.

I hate you, and I hope you die.

The cycle of emotions after discovery goes from rage, to sorrow, to compassion and back to rage. It is a roller coaster of emotions I would not wish on anyone. During this time I tried to keep my eye on my higher power, but the tsunami of mood swings swept me away.

Lights Out

Each day my affection for you diminishes.
The light dims,
It grows so faint I cannot find it in the dark.
At last it will wink out and be no more.

Then there will be everlasting dark,
      where once the clear sunlight of our union shone.

The longer my distress continued, the more I withdrew. I began to lose hope as depression took hold. I found myself in an ever-present darkness.

Carriers

What mission do they think they have,
    to spread corruption in an ever-widening path?

One touches the next,
The taint proceeds,
Arrives at last unwelcome at my door.

It was devastating to me to be infected with a disease from my own husband. This was the source of the disgust I carried toward his acting out partners. At this point, my anger toward them remained high.

II.

The Struggle to Understand

In the months following discovery, both of us began to participate in recovery activities. I have often said that going to COSA saved my life. In truth, had I not had the understanding and acceptance that the COSA fellowship gave me, my life might have ended in despair. I began to learn about addiction, and about the ways partners can be affected both before and after the discovery of addiction. I found that other women were as devastated as I was, and that some of them had broken through to a new life nonetheless. I wanted this thing called recovery.

I bought every book I could find on sex addiction, infidelity, and how to recover from them. I read them all. They helped educate me about the syndrome I was dealing with, and helped me to feel there could be solutions.

Over time, as the initial trauma lessened and I began to feel a little more like myself, I began to write about my struggle to understand what had happened to me, and to my marriage. The pain and anger were still there, but I was at least sometimes able to think about other things. My themes began to include attempts to understand how the addict thinks. At first I wasn't very good at understanding him, but I persisted.

Nevertheless, the slow progress of recovery together with being sad, traumatized and stressed for months eventually led to depression. Unfortunately, it was three years before I sought treatment for it. Before then I dragged myself to work each day, living in a mental fog. People at work wondered what was wrong with me. I was late for everything, forgetful, and sometimes confused. Eventually I lost one of the major work assignments I'd had, which led to having less salary. It was a low point, to be sure.

In 2007 things took a turn for the even-worse. I discovered that my husband had relapsed. This time I told him he needed to move out, and that we needed to be separated. He complied, and for several months he lived out of a local hotel. I began to feel as though the end was inevitable.

His work had him spending most of the week in another city anyway, so it was less of a change than one might imagine. Still, having the house, especially the bedroom, entirely to myself was freeing. I felt safer. I felt more like myself. I began to discover who I am apart from him. The three years we were separated turned out to be very healing for me. I came out stronger and less dependent on him emotionally. By 2010 I was willing to move on, if need be.

Those three years were undoubtedly difficult. My mother died. My father-in-law died. My own father became ill and came to live near me. My work remained at a low point, and I felt sad and discouraged in many ways. Even so, the separation gave me strength.

I continued to write.

Once More, With Feeling

What's that you say?
I didn't hear it.

I see your lips move,
But your soul stays silent.

There's a soundproof room in which your memories lie.
Beyond the door is a place not even you can go.
The anteroom is dark and of unknown size.

I speak into the dark,
But all I hear is an echo of my own voice
      and the sound of someone weeping.

It was hard for me to learn how shut down and emotionally closed off my husband really was. In entering therapy and recovery, one of his tasks was to open up memories and emotions he had long ago closed off, because they were too painful. Knowing that large parts of him were not accessible, even to him, was frightening for me. What terrible things could be locked away in there? Fortunately, he has done a lot of difficult work to deal with this, and is quite different now than he was when this poem was written.

Hope

I loved you in the morning of my life,
        when I was new
And hope lay on this side of the door.

Now I am no longer new.
The polish is off,
And crows have taken all the shiny pieces.

The love remains,
        but tattered, aged and worn.
The door is closed,
        and hope lies somewhere on the other side.

Often partners feel that they are now damaged goods, not good for much anymore. I felt that way, and still struggle with it now sometimes. The contrast between the hopefulness of early marriage and the uncertainty of the present is captured by the image of the closed door.

In the Mirror

I see my own eyes, hollow, dead,
Emptied of the life that loving you once brought.

Like the moon that in its phase
    turns from the sun and does not shine,
So l have lost that light
    that once came through you from love's only Source.

My face is hidden now, and dark.
Cold and stifling is the place where I await the end of night.
It will end, but not when I say, or you.

It will end when Light Eternal breaches the high wall
    that you have built around my heart.

And on that day, when perfect love arises,
    sweeping all the darkest corners clean,
There will be nothing left of you or me,
    and we will know at last what Heaven means.

This poem starts by describing the depression that had gripped me as the initial searing pain wore off and deep sadness took its place. However, it also captures hope that spiritual growth through reliance on my higher power will eventually bring healing.

Circling the Drain

You've brought me here where you have been:
Lift the lid and drop me in.
This is where you've put me, so
          push the handle, down I go.

Sometimes as I wrote about my pain, humor came up. Humor can capture ideas very pointedly, as the metaphor in this poem shows. At the same time, humor can be very healing, especially if we can laugh at things that hurt.

Excerpts from the COSA Joke Book:

Q.: How many SA's does it take to screw in a light bulb?
A.: Only one, but then he can't stop doing it.

The Sad Case of the Permanent Cure

There once was a fellow from Texas,
Who picked up some whores in his Lexus;
They mugged him in bed,
And he fell on his head,
Now he can't remember what sex is.

With Apologies to Jeff Foxworthy

You might be an SA if…

   …you think Bill Clinton was "just misunderstood".

   …you tell people that you read "Hustler" for the articles.

   …on the weekend you like to get arrested, just so you can
      meet girls.

   …you think "chickpeas" and "nut butter" sound like delightful
      new sexual experiences.

...you keep running into Charlie Sheen.

...you think mud wrestling and pole dancing should be
Olympic events.

...there are places where no one recognizes you unless you take
your pants off.

More humor. Sometimes it's just easier to laugh than to cry.

Free Fall

Step out upon the air with me;
Look! I will hold your hand.
Together we will take that step
        that leads down into an unknown land.

Before us lies the rushing wind; behind us lies the fire.
Held in the palm of God's cupped hand, we fall
Toward a landscape made from sorrow
        and desire.

This, one of my favorite short poems, is an invitation to the addict to join with the partner in taking the risk of working toward a new life.

Ghost Ship

In the night I see your sails,
Well-trimmed and white, decks spotless,
     and your brass rails gleaming.
Here are pennants, snapping high above an empty bridge:
No captain stands to steer this ship.
You are not moored to any dock, but wander,
     strangely adrift, within the arms of my harbor.
You ride high in the water, for the usual reason:
No cargo fills your hold but only shadows.
Empty you will sail, without a port and rudderless,
     until your True Captain comes, walking to you across the waves.

Addressed to the addict, this poem is about emptiness. Often the addict may look good on the outside, be functional in a day to day context, yet be without an inner life that is emotionally honest. Without a spiritual direction such as recovery can provide, the addict remains "rudderless".

On the Brink

The sleeper does not wake
        but walks a distance in his sleep.
He wanders, and his feet find the abyss.
On the edge he stops and staggers, sways, and leans over emptiness.
And still he does not wake.

Dim ghosts of emotion play across his face:
In dream he walks another path than this.
One further step and he is gone,
        vanished in the darkness far below he falls,
Arms outstretched in welcome as the bottom rises to meet him.

Several poems address my growing understanding of the addict and the mental states associated with addiction. This one uses the metaphor of sleepwalking to capture the powerlessness of the addict against the cycles of addiction.

Sentinel

Here am I, in the road, in your path,
      like the ghost of Jacob Marley come to warn.
Hiding my transparent arms within my rags,
      my chains clanking silently,
I cower in a cold wind only I can feel
      and soundlessly mouth words that no one hears.

I am a feeble kind of specter.
Who stationed me to turn you back from this, your chosen path?

It is my image that lies before you, terrible and impotent at once.
An image only:
Not the reality you might have come to know.

What kind of obstacle is this that tears to tattered mist
      at the touch of your outstretched hand?
If you would follow down that path
      no mere image can prevent your passage.

This is a poem about my own powerlessness. I came to realize that no matter how injured I was, no matter how I might show him the impact of his addiction on me, my pain, by itself, could never be enough to keep him from his self-destructive behaviors. The impetus would have to come from within him.

Execution

Such a fool I was, all this time:
Dancing on the trapdoor
With the noose about my neck.

I didn't see it coming, like a sharpened blade,
     swung wide and deadly toward my throat
By a dear, familiar hand.

Who would have known the last rites I received
Were given in the sacrament of marriage?

Self-blame is very common among partners: Why didn't I know before? What was wrong with me that I let this happen? How could I trust someone who was so untrustworthy? In my case the pain was sharpened by the fact that we underwent not one but two commitment ceremonies (wedding, vow renewal) that made no difference to my husband's addiction. Humiliated, I castigated myself for not recognizing this and allowing it to happen. Now, of course, I know that addicts are extremely good at hiding the truth. The reason that I didn't know was that my husband didn't want me to know and went to great lengths to make sure I didn't.

Eulogy

My J. is dead.
He was a good man.

Both gentle and strong,
Known for his kindness and generosity.
He was a man who loved his family,
        his country, and his God.
He abhorred evil and injustice of all kinds.
He protected the very young and honored the old;
He earned their respect and their love.

He gave value to his employer:
His fairness and honesty were a watchword,
His diligence and productivity were legend.
Those around him sought his advice and his leadership,
        and often, too, his friendship.

He loved his wife.
He valued her life's work and gave her the freedom to pursue it.
He respected her strength, and bore patiently with her weaknesses.
He nurtured in her an attitude of loving trust.

He loved his daughter above all else,
And he would have given his life to protect her from harm.

If he had a fault, it was that he worked too hard.
He did not always leave room in his life for relaxation, or in his heart
for joy.
His family did not always feel his love,
        and an emptiness grew in their hearts from his long absence.

Still, they knew that he loved them, and that what he did,
     he did for them.
They grieved at his going out,
     and rejoiced at his return.

My J. is dead.
He was a good man. He will be missed.

One of the greatest losses with discovery of a marriage-shattering addiction is the partner's loss of the positive image of the addicted person. Someone who used to seem to be a wonderful person, admirable in many ways, is suddenly re-evaluated in light of the devastating new information. Who is this person, and what has he done with my husband? It is not unlike being widowed, in some ways. The loss of the partner we thought we had must be grieved and accepted before there is hope for the creation of a new relationship.

Mother

Blessed ignorance,
That country to which you now return,
Remains inaccessible to me.

There will be a time not long from now
        when you will see its shores
And glimpse the One
Whose love awaits you there.

How I wish I could go with you!
Where time no longer matters and no memories remain
        to break my heart.

At the same time that I was struggling with the pain of my husband's addictive behaviors and their effects on me, I was also dealing with my mother's decline into Alzheimer's. Watching a loved one recede into a place where you can't follow, to lose them even though they are still physically present, is a deep loss. I started grieving for my mother several years before she actually died, and that sadness is reflected here. At the same time, it is sometimes said that ignorance is bliss. At times I wished I did not know what I knew...

I still desire your touch, and yet and yet
The night brings pictures that I can't forget.
I reach to touch your face but all the while,
I hear the lie that hides behind your smile.

Through all the pain I find I love you still;
I love the you I know, and always will;
I cannot love, nor can I even try,
The monstrous thing that smiles behind the lie.

This little rhyming poem is another of my favorites. It captures in just a few words the partner's dilemma: the awareness of evil in combination with someone long beloved. How can I reach out to you, be intimate again, when I can't avoid the memories?

Broken

Shattered pieces scattered on the floor
Carefully swept up:
First in the dustpan,
Then, laid out and cleaned,
Piece by piece, turned and placed,
To find the way they once fit together.

Somehow, they never make the whole again.
Always, there are tiny shards, fine and sharp,
Lost in corners and beneath the hiding places of shadow.
There is no point in trying to find them.
Did no one tell you?
Tears make poor adhesive,
And some things don't mend.

For the partner, not just the relationship but also the self can seem broken.

Endings

One deep and telling breath
Then I am gone:
Breathed out at last to join the unseen throng.

When I am gone
What comfort will you find
To hold together body, spirit, mind?
What substitute, demonic or divine,
Will fill the place on earth that once was mine?
I wonder if you'll soon forget my face,
Whose kiss will trace the paths mine used to trace?

The little scraps you left for me to sup
I cannot bear to think of giving up.
When I am gone I hope I cannot see
What pleasure you may find replacing me.

This poem speaks to the feeling of being replaceable, like something used up and thrown away. I continued to feel like this, and on some days I still struggle with this feeling.

Forgetting

And so when you forgot me was it like
A brilliant flash of light
So bright that it obliterated everything I am?
Bright enough that in a single flash
It burned away your memory of my name
And turned the picture of my face to ashes?

Or was it like a creeping fog
Cold, silent, deadening,
That came upon you slowly,
Robbing you of memory and thought,
Leaving in their place
An empty space in which my voice was not even an echo?

The partner cannot help but ask, "What were you thinking?!" But of course the addict was not thinking. This poem was my attempt to picture a state of mind in which one's life partner becomes temporarily invisible.

III.

A Higher Power

Many of the poems so far make reference to a higher power. An account of my journey would not be complete without a description of the way it affected my relationship with the God of my understanding. As I see it, in times of great crisis and loss, one has at least two choices. One can become angry at God, saying "Why did you do this to me?", or even lose belief in God altogether, because "a good God would never let this happen." An alternative is to lean upon your higher power for help, to try your best to turn it over to your higher power rather than trying to control the situation. My instinct was to do the latter. Now, I was by no means perfect at it! Like most partners, I tried hard to control my way through the situation, especially at first.

Later on, particularly during the time of separation, I began to let go and stopped concerning myself with what my husband was doing, and instead focused on what I was doing. I left it to my higher power to decide the outcome. I began to pray simply that His will be done. I knew for a fact that *my* will hadn't turned out so well.

As I depended more and more on my higher power, I began to feel a safety and support I had not felt before. My church became a "safe place" for me. Also, I developed the conviction that addiction is not merely a medical disease, or a mental illness, but also a spiritual condition. It seemed to me that the struggle was occurring on several levels – including some that were definitely above my pay grade! I became convinced of the reality of evil in the world. This struggle, a larger battle between good and evil, is depicted in several poems.

During this time I gradually saw my husband's struggle for recovery play out. The separation got his attention, and it made him seek recovery in a renewed way. I began to see that many of the things I thought I knew to be true of him before discovery were, in fact, still true. My worldview gradually healed as I became able to discern truth from falsehood.

Contest

Hell was laughing on the day we met.
The Angel said:
They will have joy, in measure, and their times of testing.

The Demon said:
I will put distance between them that will grow into a
*   chasm too great to cross.*
I will give them suffering to last their lives.

And the Angel said:
They will have love that binds them into one
*   and gives them strength to pass through fire.*

The Demon said:
He will have a secret vice that eats away like acid at their love,
*   and leads him down to that place from which there is no returning.*

But the Angel said:
Through her he will catch a glimpse of Light that will illuminate all secrets
*   and a taste of tears that will wash away all corruption.*

The Demon said:
I will give her loneliness and grief, and despair so great her soul will be a
wasteland.
She will long for death.

But the Angel said:
She shall have the sustenance of faith and the grace of true compassion,
That will bring her safely through this night
She will long to see the face of God.

The Demon said:
I will take him.

And the Angel said: *We will take him back, for he was never yours.*

This poem captures most clearly the theme of a battle between good and evil. It also depicts my growing conviction that not just my marriage but my husband's very soul hung in the balance.

Voice of God

In the night: Your voice, infinitely loud,
      yet to me, indistinct.
I cannot hear what You say, nor feel Your gentling touch.
There is a roaring in my head that drowns out all else,
      and my ears are stopped with the sound of my own wailing.

You turn my face toward You, and still I cannot see.
I am too small to look into the light,
      too weak to hear You speaking.

In moments when we most need our higher power, sometimes we are unable to hear him. It is our own desperate attempts to hold on and control that get in the way. At this point I was not completely ready to admit my powerlessness.

Ascent

At the foot of the hill he lies, overcome, his face turned away,
     his mouth full of dust.
From where he lies the hill looms high, its surface barren,
     a grey waste of scree and pebbles.

Slowly, painfully he rises, gains first his knees, his hands,
     then at last his feet.
Beginning his ascent he plants one step, then another,
     feels shifting gravel underfoot and slides a little, backwards.
Catching with his hands, he stops the downward slide.

Once more, starting, he ascends now with feet and hands,
     grasping at prominences, holding fast where he can,
And making forward progress in small increments.
His pack grows heavy, and he lays it down.
Possessions once treasured are abandoned to the choice:
He must continue.

Further up the slope the sun becomes his enemy.
He hangs his head and seeks to hide from its pitiless illumination:
In its light he can be clearly seen,
     splayed against the hill, his shape unmistakable.
Crows (or are they vultures?) stoop to mock him
     and to peck the naked surface of his shoulders.

Near the summit now, the goal in sight, he turns and looks behind:
The way he came is long and narrow,
There are broken places in the path,
And now he cannot see how it was possible to traverse them.

Above lies something bright.

He stumbles to his feet and reaches,
    grasping at things he cannot see but knows are there.
Dimly he hears voices, some ahead calling,
    others behind urging him on.

Here at last he loses footing, slides upon his face,
    until only his hands remain atop the hill.
Gasping, he digs at the earth with bloody, broken nails
    and struggles to arrest his fast descent.
And he is falling.
Until a hand comes, grasps his wrist, and stops his fall.

For a long moment he hangs, dependent from this hand
    that effortlessly pulls him up and to the top.
Standing face to face at last with Him whose hand it is, he rejoices.

And then the climber hears the words he never knew he longed to hear:
Welcome; Welcome home.

This is a poem of hope. The climber is of course the addict, but it could just as well be a partner, too. The climb is long and hard, and we will not make it without relying on our higher power.

Dancehall

In Hell there is a dancehall lit with flames.

In the dim and flickering light
    men shuffle in and take their seats,
Looking neither to the right nor to the left and squinting in the smoky air.
It is as dark within as outside in the night.

At the center of the room there is a stage
And down it troop in lax formation women dressed in tattered costumes.
Empty-eyed, they pose and simper, pout and grin, beckon and feint,
Their bodies covered, barely, with gold and sequined rags.
Behind them plays a sad kind of music:
A thumping beat with only one note.

Below the dancers, in their seats the men sit watching,
Each silently absorbed, each entirely alone.
Not one speaks to another,
But only soft moans and whimpers issue from their lips.
The women beg for their attention
And display themselves with the promise of more,
Each one urging, Choose me! Take me! while writhing in an agony of desire.
And every now and then a man will rise, and lunging from his seat,
    reach to pull a dancer from the stage.
But as he does, his reaching hands grasp nothingness.
The dancer's painted lips pass through his face,
    and he is left with only emptiness, and laughter from a source he
    cannot see.

The lights go down; the men file out,
      and in a moment all begins again.
Who can say when it will end, or if it will,
Or if an eternity would be enough to spend the currency of lust?
The dancers and the men themselves don't know.
The sentence they serve out is curious and strange,
      an endless cycle played and played again.
And even they may suffer unaware, not knowing
Which the demons,
Which the damned?

Is there a special hell for unrepentant sex addicts? Who knows? If there were, it might be something like this.

Gift

Now, in this twilight between waking and sleep,
My heart, overburdened, fills with tears.
Grief, blackest river, flows deep and sluggish through my dreams,
And on its banks I wander,
     watching dim shapes moving on the farther shore.
I see these scattered footprints and I know them for my own:
Everything that's happened in my life has happened here.
But here I must perform the long, slow work that is my life,
Weighed down and bent by a burden that I never knew I carried.
There is no rest until the thing is done,
And I accept at last with weary, grateful heart
     the intolerable gift that You have given me.

There came a point when I realized that maybe, just maybe, this whole horrible experience was a gift. Could it be that without this experience, I would fail to learn or develop or act in a way that my higher power intended?

IV.

Downstream

Many things changed in 2010. It was a year when I felt ready to take on the next level of challenges and independence in my life. I started new endeavors at work, which were ultimately successful. I prepared myself with information, should I need to divorce. I felt stronger than ever before, despite the many uncertainties I faced.

Then in September of 2010, almost exactly six years after I became ill, my husband was stricken with a life-threatening chronic illness. He came home from one of his lengthy trips and was so ill that I knew he had to go to the hospital immediately. It was a good thing he went, because he would likely have died otherwise. After a year of coping with this illness and trying to continue working, he was in the hospital again severely ill. He had to make the difficult decision to retire early, because his survival depended on it; the stress of working at his usual pace was incompatible with keeping his disease under control.

We both learned several things from this experience. He learned the role that work played in his addictive behaviors, and that recovery must include changing this habitual pattern. This was a very difficult loss for him, and I respect his decision to make it. I learned that despite everything that had happened, when his life was at risk, there was no question in my mind about whether I wanted to be there for him: I did. He was not going to die on my watch, if there was any way to prevent it. One could make an argument that I was being codependent in thinking this way. But I prefer to think my higher power was reminding me what was important to me. The bottom line was that he matters to me, no matter what. My love for him was unconditional, even if my being his wife *was* conditional.

The years that have followed have seen us face a variety of challenges as a family. My husband stayed at my side through my mother's death, the slow, terrible decline of my father and the heartbreaking work of cleaning out my parents' house. I stayed with him through painful tests and treatments. We walked together through our daughter's marriage and the birth of her first child. He has stayed in recovery. How do I know? I can never know for certain, but I do know he is very different than he used to be. We continue to work on restoring our intimacy as a couple.

The poems that follow largely reflect my moving to a place of greater detachment from the trauma I experienced and a desire to examine larger themes. Their content is not much like the raw feelings expressed just after discovery. They are more thoughtful and less painful. I hope you will find them illuminating.

Ursa Major Speaks

That's my daughter your hand is on, boy.
Listen now, I won't repeat this:
The hand you touch her with had best be clean.
I'm not giving you another chance.

I've seen what happens when a hand, tainted with corruption
Touches innocence and leaves its mark
Do that only once, here, and you do it no more.

Where there is no one who protects
No one who sees and who can recognize the signs,
There is no defense.
I know it now:
Innocence is not a shield.

His eye is on the sparrow, but mine is on you.

See you don't forget.

I recall thinking, as soon as I knew why I was in the hospital, in pain, "I must protect my child." A number of decisions I made afterward were to keep her as safe as possible, under the circumstances. Since she was already growing into adulthood, she was at risk for making the same mistakes I made. I now saw the world as a more dangerous place than before. This poem, addressed to a potential suitor, expresses the desire of "mother bear" to protect her child.

Rings

These rings mean nothing any more.
(*They mean everything.*)
They burn my fingers; I can't bear to have them on.
(*I can't bear to have them off.*)
They look like empty glitter now.
(*I'm the one that's empty now.*)

To wear them is painful and humiliating.
(*Not to wear them is worse.*)
Why did you give them to me?
(*They're mine and no one else's.*)

Contradictory feelings can persist for a long time. I found that my wedding rings were both a trigger to me and at the same time very precious. During the time I was separated I didn't wear them. I do now, because my feelings about them have changed.

Pile

I can't see your face.

A great and stinking pile lies in between us. Its stench fills my nose
And your voice, calling me, is muffled by its bulk.
It looms above me, higher than your head,
        and my poor shovel makes no difference.

Climbing over to you I find few footholds
Other than mementos of the happy past, half buried, smeared with filth.
Grinning faces leer within the pile, seductive and beckoning;
Their charms are lost on me.
I step on many as I climb, but more arise, clamoring for attention,
        jeering as they speak your name.

Their voices follow me.
On the other side I find you, looking up at me from where you kneel.
Filth covers your arms up past the elbows
        and I see that some is even smeared around your mouth.
I look away in silence, unable to bear the sight of you.

And now I find that, having climbed the pile,
My once clean hands are now no longer clean.
Bits and pieces, smears and trickles of the filth
Adhere in places I'd have never thought to find them.
I carry them with me from this place, unable to leave them behind,
Just as I cannot abandon you.

The sense of disgust related to my husband's acting out behaviors became quite a struggle for me. When early in my journey I tried to understand — and also tried to control—I ended up seeing more things than were healthy for me to see, particularly online. If you're not a frequent consumer of such material, it can be not only shocking but also traumatizing. Certain images and thoughts stayed with me a long time, and they made me feel both unsafe and unclean.

Suspicion

There are vermin in this house, I know it.
Sometimes late at night I hear their soft, persistent scratching in
the walls,
           their voices just outside the range of hearing.

They think I do not hear them, but I do.
And sometimes from the corner of my eye I catch
           the merest glimpse, a tail,
That disappears around a corner in the hall,
           and leaves no afterimage in my eye.

There are signs:
Disturbances in dust,
Faint prints of footsteps lingering on the stairs.
A sudden feeling of unease,
A cold, swift breeze where none should be.
And then the silence - oh, the silence!
Punctuated by bursts of purest nothingness,
Embodied *absence,*
So much more solid than the things I hear and see.

I know they're here:
They leave the faintest stench that hangs about the flowers by the door,
And in the mirror now, sometimes, I see a face that's not my own.
I hear them when I sleep:
The click and tap of claws upon the floor, a gurgling exhalation of decay,
And the crisp, dry whisper of leathery wings.

*The fear that your partner will act out again, re-traumatizing you, can be
very troubling. This poem captures the feeling of paranoia and unsafety in
the metaphor of a haunting. Indeed, I was haunted by thoughts and images
for a very long time.*

Where is Jack the Ripper when we need him?
Lost in anonymity in the far, dim reaches of the late 19th century.
Oh, but if only he were here –
What a smorgasbord of opportunities would meet his eye!
No longer limited to prowling filthy alleys in the dark to find his prey,
He could order them up by phone, like pizza.
[Would you like extra disease with that, sir?]
Or better still, patrol the Internet,
Lure them in with promises of money, love or maybe simply shame,
The thing they all come for, anyway.

So many millions clamoring for him, and what he offers them!
Till he appears, their savior with a scythe,
They must make do with other, lesser deaths.

Come soon, Jack!
Your people wait for you.
So many drops of blood as yet unspilled,
And so much work to do.

Lest anyone think that years of recovery are not occasionally disrupted by moments of rage, I offer this poem. Today's media make it easier than ever to fall prey to sex addiction. The purveyors of pornography and related things offer spiritual death that is just a click or a credit card away. Alas, many are drawn in.

The Vampire's Wife

At first, of course, I thought it was romantic:
You, climbing through my window in the night,
          overwhelming me with passion and departing before the dawn.
You drank from me, and I could see I gave you life - I, alone.
But with every time you drank I grew weaker,
          emptied of myself and filled with you.

Life with you was not what I expected.
You made me wear that long, white dress because you liked it.
You said I couldn't get a job,
          because I had to be awake for you at night.
It wasn't easy: The neighborhood dogs howling at all hours;
The excuses to the neighbors for why you were never there.

Some people knew.
They asked me, didn't I want to be free?
But by then, I had no more desires that did not find their origin with you.
When you desired to drink from me, I desired to give you what you
wanted.

You said you couldn't help it.
Something happened to you long ago that made you what you are.
You said you'd try to give it up, and I thought perhaps you would.
You started waking in the late afternoon before the sun had set.
(You wore a hat and sunscreen for me, what a man!)
And you switched to eating hamburgers, very, very rare.

But there were other things:
The bits of grave dirt clinging to your pants leg,
A tiny smear of blood upon your collar.
Then I knew.

When they came for you I stood and watched.
I did not lift a hand, or raise my voice to warn you,
Because, of course, I *had no* will:
It was day, and you were sleeping.
But when they drove the stake into your heart I felt your agony, and
screamed.

And then I tried to save you, I suppose; I don't know why.
If I could save you, wouldn't I have done it long before?

The vampire is a perfect metaphor for addiction. Partners can be drawn into the dance of dysfunction so easily, giving up the self to maintain the relationship. We can be left empty and powerless, unable to act to change our lives.

State of the Union

Like an old Chevy
With a bent frame and flood damage
It wobbles down the street,
Paint job intact,
Darkened windows rolled up tight.
It's a classic, people say, look what great condition it is in,
And how it rides so smoothly, like a dream.
Its owner keeps it clean and polished.
None of them have ever sat inside,
Felt the way the steering pulls, jerking suddenly to one side,
Or heard the radio, which switches without warning
        from one station to the next,
Traveling in an instant from the Sunday Praise Hour to Howard Stern
        and back again.
They haven't seen the back seats,
With stains that won't come out,
Or smelled what happens when the temperature gets high,
And the river water deep inside awakens from its slumber.

The marriage of a couple in recovery from the effects of sex addiction may look different from the outside than from the inside. I can recall a time just before we separated, when my husband and I were leading couple groups and appearing to be doing very well. Alas, the truth was otherwise. The old car has a good paint job, but the inside? Well…

Legacy

In the beginning: who knows whose hand drew back,
And in a moment of careless evil struck
Sending some small soul reeling, unable to stop
     from tumbling down an unchosen path,
A legacy of hate and fear,
Careening madly into subsequent generations.
The origin is lost in time,
But now the same blow reappears,
Struck again and again across the decades
Multiplying, spreading loss and terror,
Till there is no one left who recalls it could be otherwise.

How does the early trauma that leads to addiction get started? I've always said that family dysfunction is the gift that keeps on giving down the generations, until someone finally says, "It stops here!" This poem was intended to capture the tragedy of abuse that travels down the decades, damaging lives as it goes.

Tuesday Morning with the Queen

Winsome and then some,
Winnie in her chair -
Her *stroller,* meant for strolling,
Like a despot on parade.
Borne by her attendants (Lourdes, there from 8 to 4)
And waving to her subjects in the crowd
(Two joggers and a miniature schnauzer, gray),
One hand raised in sticky benediction:
Fine preparation for a life of taking bows.

In thinking about the legacy of dysfunction that leads to adult problems such as addictions, I began sketching out poems about children. This one and the one that follows are from that effort. This poem is about false empowerment – the child who is destined for a life of overindulgence and entitlement, which is also abuse.

Radio Silence

From the back seat he strains to hear them speak.
Just a word, a chuckle or a smile will do;
Anything to break the impasse.
He cannot hear a thing; he has not now for thirty days or more.
How do they do it?
How do they wander in their orbits, coming close but never
intersecting?
Perhaps, he thinks, they use some frequency he cannot hear,
    like the hiss between the stations on the radio.
He wonders: Is this the price of growing up?
Will this be what he is, when he is grown?
A statue of a man, blanketed in chilly isolation,
    and a silence like the space between the stars.

Children struggle to make sense of dysfunctional adult relationships, and often learn the wrong things from what they observe. Emotional disconnection is learned early as a way to avoid feeling.

Envy

The ones I envy are not the great beauties,
Not the well-dressed ones with shining hair and long legs
Not the ones that draw the eye,
But the short ones, the round and wrinkled ones,
With gray hair and comfortable shoes
Whose husbands look at them with love
     and hold their hands with tenderness.
The ones whose husbands linger at their bedsides at the end of life,
And whose passing is marked with deepest grief
And a sense of irreplaceable loss.

After some recovery I discovered that what I most desired was the sense of safety and intimacy, of being unconditionally loved, that I used to have. I watched my late father spend his own last years caring for my mother as she was gradually taken by dementia. It was extremely difficult for him, and it was a clear example of unflagging devotion. I had always hoped for the same kind of devotion in my marriage, but the discovery of addiction shattered that dream. Over time I have regained some of that feeling, in part due to my growing awareness that the addiction was never about me, and in part because of the ways my husband has demonstrated the fruits of his recovery.

The Bargain

This is not what I signed on for.

The recruiting poster had a nice young man, smiling, holding out his
hand,
And underneath it said, "Get married, see the world!"
And next to that, The Good Housekeeping Seal of Approval.
There must be some mistake.
Somewhere there must have been another poster
      with a seedy, grim-faced man, half-obscured in shadow,
        one hand inside his own trench coat, the other reaching, grasping.
And underneath it must have said,
"Here, little girl, would you like some candy?"
And next to that no seal at all, except a bloody handprint.

They must have switched the papers when I signed.
I must have boarded the wrong bus, taken the wrong exit.
And that must be why I ended up where I don't belong
      and why
This is not my life.

One of the feelings I most struggled with was a sense of having been tricked
or cheated. That's what betrayal is, of course. I kept wanting to wake up and
find this was all a big mistake.

Happy Anniversary

Thanks for all you've given me over the years.

Thank you for your callous disregard for my feelings and my welfare;
It forced me to re-examine how much I was depending on you.
Thank you for making me feel so unloved, and so unlovable;
It made me realize you are not the source of my worth.
Thank you for threatening my health;
It reminded me that I am responsible for protecting myself.
Thank you for allowing me to see how little you understood about
        yourself, and about me;
It helped me to begin to have understanding and compassion toward you.
Thank you for telling me the ugly truth about yourself;
It brought me to the realization that I would rather have the truth with
        pain,
than live in a world of deception.
Thank you for leaving me humiliated and devastated;
From this I learned that I could survive even the worst that life has to offer.
Thank you for breaking your vows to me;
It helped me to discover what I will and will not accept, and where my
        boundaries lie.
Thank you for failing to protect the well-being of my child;
I now know there are things worth sacrificing myself for, and this is one
        of them.
Thank you for showing me how much you had been hurt;
I came to see that I do not have to hurt you anymore.
Thank you for pursuing your recovery as though your life depends
        on it—
Because it does.
Thank you for humbling yourself enough to ask for and accept help;
It helped me to realize my own need for help.
Thank you for listening to me, even when my words made you feel
        frightened and ashamed;

By doing that you showed me how much I matter to you.
Thank you for taking responsibility for your own actions instead of
        blaming them on me;
In this way you first opened the door to forgiveness.
Thank you for acknowledging your need for God's grace and mercy;
You are a constant reminder to me that I need them, too.

Thank you for remaining my husband. I love you.
Happy Anniversary.

This poem is left for last in this book because it portrays the hard lessons that I, as a partner, have learned from my journey. These were costly lessons, but I now hold them dear, because they are the heart of my recovery. My husband's recovery played a role in mine, as well. As he grew and changed, my ability to be in a relationship with him was gradually rebuilt. Much as I sometimes hate to admit it, I am undoubtedly a better, healthier person on the other end of this experience.

Some Final Words

I would not want anyone to think that the end of these poems represents an endpoint to recovery. My journey continues. Though I am no longer writing from the heart of devastating pain, I am irrevocably changed. I have consciously tried to choose life and growth over hatred and despair. Though I am not always successful, this choice is essential to my recovery.

I wish you life and growth in your journey as well. Remember that however painful your feelings may be, you are not alone. May your higher power be with you through every step.

EV

Elaine VandeReis is the pen name of a partner
of a sex addict living in Texas.